PATENTS AND PUBLIC HEALTH

TWO ESSAYS ON MEDICINE & GENETICS AS INTELLECTUAL PROPERTY

MATTHEW HOWARD

2015

Paperback ISBN-10: 0692367195
Paperback ISBN-13: 9780692367193
Kindle Ebook ASIN: B00S5J5H3I

Contents

Human Genes in the Global Market:
How Two Nations Reached Opposing

Abstract
I. The Origins of Biological and Genetic Patents in the
   U.S.
II. The Origins of the Myriad Genetics Case in the U.S.
    and Abroad.
III. The Myriad Genetics Case in the U.S.
IV. The Origins of the Myriad Genetics Case in
    Australia.
V. The Decisions in the Myriad Case in Australia.
VI. Conclusion.
References

Patents and Public Health in the Age of TRIPS:
Why the Future Depends on Connecting Patent

Abstract
I. Medicine as Intellectual Property.
II. Commercial Interest versus Public Health.
III. The Consequence of Inequities between Nations.
IV. Problems and Power at the Patent Offices.
V. The Future of Patent Offices and Public Health.
References

Contents

Introduction

Now is an important time in human history. Viral outbreaks threaten lives and make headlines. We see new diseases appear and spread across the planet. We map our genetic code. And we now share the planet with lifeforms of our own creation.

A global communication system keeps us informed. But a global system of trade agreements plays a very important role we do not hear so much about. These trade agreements govern, among other things, patent protection for intellectual property.

When a nation accepts a trade agreement treating medicines as intellectual property, it can find itself ill-equipped to confront public health crises like outbreaks of viruses and disease. Genetic material, too, can become protected intellectual property, although the courts of different nations disagree on just what material and how protected it might be. Once the subject of futuristic science fiction novels, the commodification and ownership of human genetic material has become our reality in the 21st century.

The two essays in this booklet address the ethical concerns as well as the practical, administrative realities for the offices and courts where governments make decisions that affect all of us; our health, our genetic code, and our future. Thank you for reading.

Matthew
January 2015

Human Genes in the Global Market:
How Two Nations Reached Opposing Conclusions to the Myriad Genetics Case

Abstract

The Myriad Genetics cases in the United States and Australia focus on patent control of two human gene sequences and the clinical methods of detecting them. Myriad Genetics patents refer to the genes as "17q-linked breast and ovarian cancer susceptibility gene" due to their location on the long arm of human chromosome 17. They received the names BRCA1 and BRCA2 from Mary Claire King, whose group at the University of California, Berkeley identified them in published research in 1990. Myriad Genetics' subsequent patent claims on BRCA1 and BRCA2 entered litigation in the US in 2009 and Australia in 2010, and met with dispute in the European Union and Canada. The US Supreme Court issued a final decision on the validity of the patent claims in 2013, reversing an earlier decision at the Circuit Court level which had, in turn, reversed an initial decision at the District Court level. The Federal Court of Australia's appeals court reached a judgment in September 2014 upholding a Federal Court decision from 2013. While the US Supreme Court invalidated the patents covering the gene sequence, the Australian courts upheld them. The differences in both the legal precedents and the patent terminology in each country have a direct bearing on why such opposing decisions happened. The political and economic realities of today's globalized business environment also influenced the decisions. To the extent that patents help enforce intellectual property rights, understanding how each nation came to its decision provides insight into the role of human genetic material in today's global information society.

Keywords: BRCA1, BRCA2, discovery, genes, European Patent Office, Federal Court of Australia, Genetic Technologies, intellectual property, invention, litigation, Myriad Genetics, patent, US Supreme Court.

I. The Origins of Biological and Genetic Patents in the U.S.

The 2013 decision by the U.S. Supreme Court in *Association for Molecular Pathology v. Myriad Genetics, Inc.* definitively concluded four years of mixed judicial response to the case. Myriad's patents became invalid at the District Court level in 2010, but the Court of Appeals for the Federal Circuit reversed this decision, returning Myriad's patent rights to them (Supreme Court Orders, 2012, p. 26). The Supreme Court, after ordering the Court of Appeals to review and reconsider its decision in 2012, eventually reversed the decision again, striking down the patents in 2013 just three years before they would have expired (Victory for Genes, 2013, p. 792). This mixed judicial response follows a pattern of conflicting U.S. court decisions about biological material, a pattern showing distinctly different agendas between the Supreme Court and the Circuit Court.

The legality of patenting natural genetic material first came into question in 1948 in a case concerning a combination of different bacteria which, when applied to seeds, assisted in nitrogen uptake in adult plants (Leal, 2014, p. 406). The Supreme Court ruled in *Funk Brothers Seed Co. v. Kalo Inoculant Co.* that, because all of the bacteria occurred naturally, they could not be patented (ibid, p. 407). The court's decision asserted the qualities of these naturally occurring bacteria "like the heat of the sun, electricity, or the qualities of metals, are part of the storehouse of knowledge of all men... manifestations of laws of nature, free to all men, and reserved exclusively to none" (Rogers, 2013, p. 446). Patents were intended to provide protection to inventions and inventors, and the court did not consider naturally occurring biological material to be an invention.

This decision showed consistency with an earlier case regarding biological material in 1874: *American Wood Paper Co. v. Fibre Disintegrating Co.* In that case, the Supreme Court "rejected a patent for cellulose isolated from nature" on the basis that extracting a natural substance by "decomposition or disintegration of material substances" did not render that biological substance eligible for patent (ibid, p. 444). This thinking foreshadowed the Supreme Court's 2013 decision in *Myriad*, summarized by Justice Clarence Thomas: "Myriad did not create or alter any of the genetic material in the BRCA1 and BRCA2 genes. The location and order of the nucleotides existed in nature before Myriad found them. Nor did Myriad create or alter the genetic structure of DNA" (Victory for Genes, 2013, p. 792).

Ten years later, however, in the 1958 case *Merck & Co. v. Olin Mathieson Chemical Corp.*, the court ruled in favor of patenting biological material concentrated or purified from its natural state (Leal, 2014, p. 407). This decision differed from *Funk Bros.* owing to the modification of the material, in this case vitamins and adrenalin, which brought the naturally occurring material into a new form. Subtle though the difference may be, the court's decision shows consistency with their earlier thinking: discovering a natural biological material does not make the material patent eligible, but inventing new forms of it could. The crux of the matter lies in the invention, not the discovery.

Two events in the 1980s reinforced this thinking but began a new stage in the patenting of biological material and organisms. The 1980 case *Diamond v. Chakrabaty* involved the creation of a new form of bacteria, one that did not occur naturally (ibid, p. 408). Here, the Supreme Court upheld its thinking on discovery versus invention. While the Funk Bros. case involved bacteria found in nature, the newly created bacteria in *Chakrabaty* qualified as an invention. The court ruled that "anything... made by man" could be eligible for patenting (ibid, p. 408). The Supreme Court split five-to-four on the *Chakrabaty* decision, but the deciding factor was the ability of the bacteria to decompose crude oil—ability not found in naturally occurring bacteria and thus qualifying for invention (Rogers, 2013, p. 448).

In 1987, this thinking found reinforcement in *Ex parte Allen*, a challenge to a rejection of a patent involving the genetic material of oysters wherein cell nuclei could be induced to contain "multiple DNA chromosomes of the same type" (Leal, 2014, p. 408). The Board of Patent Appeals and Interference referred to *Chakrabaty* as precedent that, as an invention, genes and even whole organisms were patent-eligible. The United States Patent and Trademark Office (USPTO) issued a statement agreeing with this.

The Court of Appeals for the Federal Circuit which decided in Myriad's favor made a similar decision in 1993. In their ruling on *In re Bell*, the court disregarded the fact that DNA sequences occur naturally and reduced them to mere chemical compounds eligible for patents (ibid, p. 409). Disregarding the Supreme Court's insistence on invention rather than discovery, this court opened the doors for patents on naturally occurring genes. This move that resulted in "more than three million gene-related patents" applied for in the next ten years, "several thousand" of which the USPTO approved (ibid, p. 409). Clearly, the Court of Appeals had different ideas than the Supreme Court and did not consider invention a necessary component of patent eligibility. This attitude foreshadows the Australian court decisions regarding Myriad Genetics, and *Chakrabaty* would earn a mention in the reasoning of those decisions.

II. The Origins of the Myriad Genetics Case in the U.S. and Abroad.

During this ten-year wave of genetic patent applications, Myriad applied for a patent on BRCA genes in 1994, with an update to clarify the gene sequence in 1995 (Bosch, 2004, p. 1780). Published research from the University of California, Berkeley in 1990 had revealed "the general location of a gene linked to breast cancer" (Patent Act of 1952, 2013, p. 388). Mary Claire King led the UC team which announced their findings at the American Society of Human Genetics Meeting. Though the team identified the gene BRCA1 "on chromosome 17 through a technique called linkage analysis," researchers from the United Kingdom, France, Belgium, the Netherlands, and Canada all collaborated in attempts to map BRCA1 and BRCA2 (Gold, 2010).

Following this announcement, Mark Skolnick of the University of Utah's Centre for Genetic Epidemiology, a competing laboratory, spun off Myriad Genetics from his group in 1991 to obtain venture capital for this line of research (ibid, 2010). Myriad Genetics soon isolated BRCA1 and BRCA2. Next, they invented clinical testing methods to identify mutations in the genes relating to increased risk for breast and ovarian cancer (Patent Act of 1952, 2013, p. 388). Myriad Genetics sought to patent not only the clinical methods they invented, but the naturally occurring genetic material they discovered.

The USPTO granted Myriad patents covering 47 mutations in the BRCA1 gene in 1997, then five additional patents covering the BRCA1 gene and associated tests, and finally two patents in 1998 "covering methods of detecting BRCA1 mutations and the entire sequence of the BRCA1 gene and tools used" in Myriad's work, the last of which "covered all uses of the BRCA1 gene" (Gold, 2010). The patents positioned Myriad as the only entity with legal rights to isolate the gene itself. And since their testing methods required isolating the gene, they became the only entity with legal rights to test for it, too (Patent Act of 1952, 2013, p. 389).

The patents covering BRCA2 would come later. The Cancer Research Campaign first filed for a patent on BRCA2 in the United Kingdom, having funded research by a UK group of 40 researchers from six countries who published the gene's sequence in *Nature* in December 1995 (Gold, 2010). Just one day before this publication, however, US researchers including Mark Skolnick claimed this work was only a partial sequence and only covered six mutations of BRCA2. Skolnick's group deposited the complete sequence into a database of gene sequences (Gen-Bank), published their findings in *Nature Genetics* in 1996, and filed for US patents—patents issued by the USPTO in 1998 and 2000 (ibid, 2010). In the US, Myriad Genetics gained intellectual property control over BRCA1, BRCA2, the methods of their isolation, and the clinical tests based on the isolation.

Despite approval in the U.S., the patents met resistance overseas—not in courts, but at the European Patent Office (EPO). The EPO had granted three patents to Myriad in January 2001, but "several European research centres, along with other organizations and the European Parliament, filed a joint opposition to the patent in October 2001" (Bosch, 2004, p. 1780). The conflict stemmed not from the debate over invention versus discovery but from Myriad's denial of licenses to research the genes, and its refusal to let any laboratories but its own test DNA samples using its technology (ibid, p. 1780). The opposition called this an "abusive monopoly," and the EPO revoked the patent on May 18, 2004 (ibid, p. 1780). The revoked patent covered the diagnostic test, though the Technical Board of Appeal subsequently limited the scope of the patents on the mutations of the BRCA1 gene in 2005, and the Board greatly limited the patent over BRCA2 that year as well (Gold, 2010). The EPO did not invalidate all of Myriad Genetics' BRCA-related patents, but they greatly limited the scope of the material and testing processes involved.

Myriad Genetics also pursued patent control and licensing arrangements in Canada, but the full extent of the Canadian campaign exceeds the scope of this paper. Briefly, the Canadian province of Ontario supported local BRCA testing without regard to Myriad's patenting attempts in Canada, resulting in a highly charged political situation. At one point, the US made threats of trade sanctions against Canada. But after years of posturing, committee reviews, inflammatory letters, political spectacle, and debate, Myriad "decided to give up on the Canadian market" when they could not bully Canada into enforcing the patents (ibid, 2010). Myriad's failure to force total control over BRCA genes and testing in the European Union and Canada foreshadowed its eventual defeat in the U.S. Supreme Court.

III. The Myriad Genetics Case in the U.S.

In the U.S., opposition began in 2009 when the American Civil Liberties Union (ACLU) and the Public Patent Foundation called the constitutionality of the patents into question, filing suit against Myriad Genetics and the USPTO (Victory for Genes, 2013, p. 792). The ACLU was joined in this effort by "six nonprofit organizations that engage in research and advocacy, eight university-affiliated scientists whose work was impeded by Myriad's patents, and six individuals who were unable to obtain desired BRCA screenings because of Myriad's monopoly on testing" (Patent Act of 1952, 2013, p. 389). "The District Court for the Southern District of New York granted summary judgment for the plaintiffs in 2010," ruling against Myriad's patent claims for the composition of the BRCA genes and its testing methods (Cong, 2012, p. 755). The District Court "invalidated seven of Myriad's US patents relating to the BRCA1 and BRCA2 genes and associated genetic tests" (Gold, 2010). The judge in this case, Judge Sweet, referred to the existing Supreme Court decisions regarding naturally occurring biological material and physical phenomena (Patent Act of 1952, 2013, p. 389-90). Judge Sweet also struck down the methods claims covering the processes for clinical testing.

The Court of Appeals, however, upheld the patents, reversing the District Court's decision, and again upheld their own decision in August 2012 after the remand ordered by the Supreme Court (Cong, 2012, p. 755). The remand order from the Supreme Court considered its recent decision in *Mayo Collaborative Services v. Prometheus Laboratories, Inc.* "Prometheus, having patented a method of adjusting dosages based on patients' biological response" had sued Mayo Collaborative Services "which had developed a similar test" (Supreme Court

Orders, 2012, p. 26). In *Prometheus*, the Supreme Court unanimously found the method in question for determining dosages merely described natural laws, and Justice Breyer made it clear the court believed "granting monopolies over laws of nature through patents would impede future research rather than promote innovation" (Patent Act of 1952, 2013, p. 390). The court ruled in favor of Mayo.

The Circuit Court, ordered to reconsider their decision in this light, still did not agree. In terms of discovery versus invention, the Circuit Court's majority asserted that although the DNA in question occurred naturally, the process of cleaving the DNA and isolating it led to "distinctive chemical composition" that rendered it patent-eligible (Cong, 2012, p. 756). Specifically, the Circuit Court referred to the *Chakrabaty* decision's emphasis on biological material with characteristics different from those occurring in nature. The differing characteristic in *Myriad* was that the isolated BRCA genes lacked introns in their molecules, something they had in their naturally occurring forms, and this lack made them "especially distinctive" (Patent Act of 1952, 2013, p. 391). Judge Lourie's opinion for the majority argued that the genes in question were distinctly different from naturally occurring ones due to their separation from the larger DNA molecule in the isolation process (ibid, p. 391). The Australian courts would later favor this rationale.

While the Supreme Court reached a unanimous decision in *Mayo*, the Circuit Court found itself split on the matter (Rogers, 2013, p. 436). The dissenting opinion argued nothing about the isolation process for BRCA changed the "structure or function of naturally occurring genes," thus invalidating claims of invention and rendering the genes ineligible for patenting (Cong, 2012, p. 756). Judge Bryson's dissenting opinion argued merely separating a component of the larger DNA molecule did not render it any more eligible than a kidney could become patent-eligible upon removal from the human body, or a mineral could become patent-eligible simply because someone extracted it from the earth (Patent Act of 1952, 2013, p. 392). Despite this straightforward, common-sense reasoning, the other Circuit Court judges outvoted Judge Bryson two-to-one. The Circuit Court, in failing to acknowledge that "isolated DNA segments have the identical nucleotide sequence and the same function as native DNA" and lack both the "marked changes required under *Chakrabaty*" and the "inventive step required under *Prometheus*," disregarded "150 years of Supreme Court cases that physical phenomena found in nature and the laws of nature are not patentable subject matter" (Rogers, 2013, p. 434).

Upon the failure of this remand to invalidate the patents, the ACLU petitioned the Supreme Court to take up the case. The court "held that isolated DNA molecules are not patent eligible" and "rejected the Federal Circuit's contention that the chemical changes created during the isolation process made the molecules distinctive" (Patent Act of 1952, 2013, p. 393). The court, consistent with its historical decisions, ruled the BRCA genes "are a product of nature and therefore ineligible for patenting" (Myriad Diagnostic Concerns, 2013, p. 571). This decision was unanimous. It marked the "first time that the US Supreme Court has invalidated a human gene" patent (Victory for Genes, 2013, p. 792).

IV. The Origins of the Myriad Genetics Case in Australia.

The story of Myriad Genetics' patent litigation did not end with the U.S. Supreme Court's decision. It continued in Australia. But before the matter came to court, some interesting things happened with the Australian licensee of the BRCA patents: Genetic Technologies, Ltd (GTG). Myriad Genetics had licensed the BRCA test to GTG "because GTG was pursuing Myriad for patent infringement," and the patent conflict between the companies resolved in each gaining licensing rights to the other's DNA patents (Gold, 2010). Things became complicated in 2007 when Dr. Merv Jacobson, CEO and co-founder of GTG and its largest shareholder, retired. As reported in *Australian Life Scientist*, Jacobson, who would maintain a position as a non-executive director, had preferred <u>not</u> enforcing the company's patent rights on BRCA; instead, he called BRCA testing "GTG's gift to Australia" (O'Neill, 2009).

New CEO Michael Ohanessian decided to change this relaxed policy, a move that would mean public laboratories would "no longer be permitted to perform commercial testing on [their] patients for mutations of the genes," although the change would not block their ability to continue research on the genes (O'Neill, 2009). Dr. Jacobson objected so vehemently that he announced he would seek a resolution to remove Ohanessian and four other directors, the chairman, and three non-executive directors. The effects of this announcement included GTG's requesting the Australian Stock Exchange "halt trading of its shares" (ibid). The company backed down from its threat of enforcing "its patent rights against laboratories offering BRCA testing" in October 2008 (Cook-Deegan, 2014). Ohanessian was eventually deposed as CEO as a result of this conflict, though Dr. Jacobson also resigned soon after (O'Neill, 2009).

The conflict spurred the Australian Senate to hold "a series of hearings, and a bill proscribing DNA sequence patents was proposed, but the new government opposed it, and it lapsed" (Cook-Deegan, 2014). GTG thus enjoyed a position of benevolent power, unthreatened by any new governmental legislation regarding DNA sequences. The difference between the Australian situation and the cases in Europe, Canada, and America lies in the good will of Dr. Jacobson at GTG which could not be more different than the heavy-handed approach Myriad Genetics took to other international markets.

Dr. Jacobson, quoted in *Australian Life Scientist*, explained his position on not enforcing GTG's BRCA testing patents. Dr. Jacobson noted that government laboratories, out of fear of patent enforcement from Myriad Genetics, had begun BRCA testing but not invested in it enough to make it a timely process, and "some women were waiting up to two years, which would put them at risk of developing cancers as they waited." Because GTG won "exclusive rights to perform BRCA testing in Australia and New Zealand," they "set up a state-of-the-art laboratory, at least as good as Myriad's, that would perform BRCA testing accurately, and in much less time." The GTG labs eventually reduced the testing time to "two months" and even "as little as four weeks." Motivated to create a "socially responsible strategy," Jacobson asserted that GTG was not "Myriad's policemen" and did not obtain the patent rights "to beat up other testing laboratories... If people wanted to do BRCA testing themselves, they were free to do so, but if they wanted our help, they had that too" (O'Neill, 2009).

Despite these statements of good will from Dr. Jacobson, the conflict makes it clear that if Genetic

Technologies had wanted to enforce its patents, it had the legal right to do so—a legal right that covered both private, potential competitors and public, governmental health facilities. GTG's benevolence stemmed from the humanitarian philosophy of just one doctor, and policy could easily go the other way once he retired or moved on. This is why, in 2010, the BRCA patents entered litigation in Australian courts. It was not, as in the case of the European Patent Office, that Myriad Genetics created an abusive monopoly. It was merely the <u>threat</u> that such a state would come to pass. This is why Paul Grogan, the Director of Advocacy at Cancer Council Australia, would tell the Australian press, "In 2008, Australian women were only protected from an attempted commercial monopoly over the BRCA1 and BRCA2 tests because the company that threatened to take those tests away from public laboratories withdrew its patent claims voluntarily... There was nothing in the law to protect healthcare customers" (Corderoy, 2014). These healthcare customers began the Australian litigation.

V. The Decisions in the Myriad Case in Australia.

The organization Cancer Voices of Australia, along with cancer survivor Yvonne D'Arcy of Brisbane represented by the law firm of Maurice Blackburn, filed suit against Myriad and GTG in 2010 (Guardian, 2014). The case entered the Federal Court of Australia in Sydney, Judge Nicholas presiding (Conley, 2010). Judge Nicholas issued a decision on February 15, 2013 in favor of Myriad and GTG, dismissing all charges (Cancer Voices, 2013, p. 39). An appeals court subsequently heard the case. On September 5, 2014, its panel of five judges unanimously ruled to uphold Judge Nicholas' decision (Cook-Deegan, 2014). The appeals court—the Federal Court of Australia, New South Wales District Registry, General Division—after a lengthy discussion recapitulating the scientific and precedent reasoning of the previous court, dismissed the appeal (D'Arcy, 2014, p. 3). At the time of this paper, the case may still be appealed at one final level—the Australian High Court (Masnick, 2014). Though it may be too early to close the book and draw conclusions about the state of genetic patents in Australia, examining of the reasoning of these two Australian Federal Courts is worthwhile.

As with many of the earlier cases discussed here, Judge Nicholas examined the difference between invention and discovery. He explains, after a lengthy lesson on the fundamentals of DNA and genetic science, the reasoning behind determining "whether isolation of naturally occurring DNA and RNA results in an artificial state of affairs with a discernible effect—whether claims to isolated DNA and RNA are to a 'mere discovery' and therefore not patentable—whether claims to isolated DNA and RNA are to a 'product of nature' and therefore not patentable" (Cancer Voices, 2013). Despite the weight other courts have given to the difference between discovery and invention, the appeals court in Australia found this subject of little concern in their decision. As Dr. Robert Cook-Deegan explained, the legal reasoning of the appeals court:

> "clearly states that a distinction between invention and discovery is not a fruitful conceptual framework for patent law, and quite explicitly rejects the U.S. Supreme Court's arguments in *AMP v Myriad*. The opinion lauds Judge Lourie of the U.S. Court of Appeals for the Federal Circuit, who upheld Myriad's claims on isolated DNA molecules in two majority opinions that were unanimously reversed by the U.S. Supreme Court" (Cook-Deegan, 2014).

Dr. Cook-Deegan may be overstating the appeals court's disregard for the concept of invention versus discovery, though. Paragraphs 110-115 in the decision directly address discovery and invention, cite Australian cases going back to 1903 as precedent, and mention the U.S. cases of *Funk Bros.* and *Chakrabaty* (D'Arcy, 2014, 23-5). The court in this case, however, targeted terms more widely argued in Australian patent law; specifically "artificially created state of affairs" and "matter of manufacture," both terms somewhat unfamiliar in the U.S. but important legal concepts in Australia.

As to whether or not a manufactured item was a "product of nature" and whether or not a microorganism would be "markedly different from something that already exists in nature," the court reasoned "there was no requirement" for determining these things in Australian patent law, based on the precedents (ibid, p. 24). The court examined precedent that "invention may consist of using the material or some new adaptation of it so as to serve the new purpose. If the new use consists in taking advantage of a hitherto unknown or unsuspected property, there may be invention" (ibid, p. 24). The court determined it is "only necessary to show one inventive step in the advance made beyond the prior limits of the relevant art" (ibid, p. 25). In other words, within the context of Australian patent law, invention can mean finding a new use for an old thing, or taking previous uses and advancing them one more step.

This argument about the nature of invention and its relevance to intellectual property and patent rights is nothing new, but neither is it without criticism. The advancement of science and invention relies on methods, equipment, and knowledge of previous workers, researchers, and institutions. In the context of developing new medicines and medical treatments, "the intellectual labor that went into the drug design process did not occur from first principles; rather, in every case, the inventor's thought process was critically shaped by the cumulative insights of his or her predecessors" (Shah, p. 844). This argument does not deny the continual process of invention; rather, it denies the wisdom of granting exclusive patent control to persons, corporations, or institutions who, having stood on the shoulders of giants, now presume to extend unilateral control over products and processes that utterly depend on prior work for their existence.

Wisdom, however, did not concern the Australian appeals court, and it said so:

"This case is not about the wisdom of the patent system. It is about the application of Australian patent law, as set out in the Act and as developed by the courts since the Statute of Monopolies. It is not about whether, for policy or moral or social reasons, patents for gene sequences should be excluded from patentability. ...It is not a matter for the court, but for

Parliament to decide. Parliament has considered the question of the patentability of gene sequences and has chosen not to exclude them but to make amendments to the Act to address, in part, the balance between the benefits of the patent system and the incentive thereby created, and the restriction on, for example, subsequent research" (D'Arcy, 2014, p. 47).

If neither concern for wisdom, nor the distinction between invention and discovery, nor ethical problems with patenting products of nature informed the thinking of the court, then what did? In a word: isolation. First, based on the testimony of genetic scientists quoted at length in the decision by Judge Nicholas, the court decided the isolated portions of the DNA molecule in Myriad's isolated BRCA material are chemically "different to the gene comprising the nucleic acid sequence as it exists in nature" (ibid, p. 49). Counter arguments from depositions and testimonies cited in the decision assert the genetic information encoded was still the same, and the chemical changes noted by the court merely resulted from the molecule's separation from its natural place in the chain. The Australian court did not find these counter arguments compelling enough to sway its decision. It stands in opposition to the opinion from Supreme Court Justice Clarence Thomas which states "We... hold that genes and the information they encode are not patent eligible... simply because they have been isolated from the surrounding genetic material" (Victory for Genes, 2013, p. 792).

The court further determined "isolation of the nucleic acid also leads to an economically useful result—in this case, the treatment of breast and ovarian cancers" (D'Arcy, 2014, p. 49). Determining the creation of "economically useful results" plays a significant role in Australian patent law. Plus, while the Supreme Court might find a product of nature ineligible for patent, the Australian court found excluding products of nature "is not in accordance with the principles of patent law in Australia and has been specifically rejected as a reason for exclusion in" a precedent-setting case (ibid, p. 50).

This precedent comes from 1959's *National Research Development Corporation v Commissioner of Patents* which "requires that an invention apply to an 'artificially created state of affairs'" (Cook-Deegan, 2014). As Dr. Robert Cook-Deegan explained, "this criterion in effect means that if 'we did it in our lab' it will clear the threshold for patent eligibility. Given this precedent, the Federal Court's ruling is sensible" (ibid, 2014). The genetic material isolated in Myriad Genetics' processes "has resulted in an artificially created state of affairs for economic benefit," and therefore "is properly the subject of letters patent" that meets the requirements of section 18(1) of Australia's Patent Acts 1990 (D'Arcy, 2014, p. 50).

Thus, the two Australian courts decided in favor of the patent-eligibility of Myriad's clinical testing processes and the piece of genetic material the tests isolate from human DNA, given the slight chemical change (absence of introns) that happens in the isolation process. The Australian courts believe this subtle distinction does not threaten to extend patent control to the human genome itself either in part or in whole. As Judge Nicholas noted in his original decision,

> "There is no doubt that naturally occurring DNA and RNA as they exist inside the cells of the human body cannot be the subject of a valid patent. However, the disputed claims do not cover naturally occurring DNA and RNA as they exist inside such cells. The disputed claims extend only to naturally occurring DNA and RNA which have been extracted from cells obtained

from the human body and purged of other biological materials with which they were associated" (Cancer Voices, 2013, p. 38-9).

Dr. Cook-Deegan argued this rationale about isolation, however, is a "lawyer's trick" that creates patent infringement on the part of anyone attempting to analyze DNA molecules containing the BRCA sequences; and, the imprecise nature of defining isolated genetic material—as opposed to the same material in its original place in the DNA molecule—will block any researcher's ability to access, understand, or experiment on these cancer-associated mutations without being subject to potential litigation (Cook-Deegan, 2014). Myriad's patent claims include "broadest method claims" giving them "exclusive rights to any way of comparing the DNA sequence from a sample to the reference sequence of the BRCA1 and BRCA2 genes disclosed in Myriad's patents" (Cook-Deegan, 2013, p. 298). This means the patents, as upheld by the Australian case, at least, extend to merely comparing a DNA sample to the known (and naturally occurring) BRCA sequences. In other words, a public health facility or private laboratory cannot even compare a sample to a piece of discovered human DNA without infringing the patent. Or, to put it in simplest terms: *Do not even look at it.* It is difficult to imagine how such utter control over genetic research activities can possibly benefit innovation, despite proponents of the Australia decision rallying around the judgment as a victory for medical and genetic innovation.

VI. Conclusion.

These concerns may well be met and resolved in the Australian High Court, or they may not. Either way, the story will not end there. Each nation has its own patent laws. Each nation potentially faces this same time-consuming and costly journey through the judicial system to arrive at its own conclusions. Australia and the U.S. have cooperated extensively on creating mutual trade agreements to cover intellectual property rights and patent rights. But their opposing decisions on the Myriad Genetics cases demonstrate patent laws on biological materials and the human genome have not yet reached the level of international standardization aimed for by instruments like the World Trade Organization's TRIPS and TRIPS-plus agreements. If such a standard already existed, such as ones developing for pharmaceutical products, software, and other forms of intellectual property, the U.S. Supreme Court and the Federal Court of Australia would not find themselves so diametrically opposed on such a fundamental concern.

Patents, as a means of claiming property rights to produce financial gain, involve the economic incentives for knowledge production. Is patent protection of knowledge necessary to drive the innovation required for growth and technological advancement in today's information society? No clear consensus exists. As one Australian patent lawyer said in response to the September ruling by the appeals court, "This decision is also certainly not going to stifle research and innovation in this field; in fact, I wonder if we will see more U.S. companies starting to try to commercialise things here" (Corderoy, 2014). This echoes a belief held by some in the U.S. that the Supreme Court's ruling is "the latest of a series of reverses to the intellectual property (IP) foundations needed to support innovative diagnostic enterprises" (Myriad Diagnostic Concerns, 2013, p. 571).

Such arguments miss the finer point: the distinction between patenting innovative processes for researching genetic material and clinically testing it, versus patenting the genetic material itself. This is the wisdom in Judge Bryson's opinion at the U.S. Circuit Court level. Judge Bryson understood that innovation and invention reside in new ways of doing things, new technologies, new processes and methods, new equipment and products. These are the things that patents were meant to cover, not the human genome, and not naturally occurring phenomenon. Judge Bryson understood this point, the Supreme Court came to understand it, and the European Patent Office and Canada also understood it. All of them have invalidated, ignored, or severely restricted the kind of patent rights Myriad Genetics and its licensees have tried so vigorously to assert for more than a decade now in their nations.

One might suspect the Australian courts understood the distinction as well, but brushed it aside to create a climate where U.S. corporations would feel encouraged to bring new businesses and new streams of revenue to their nation. As one of the leading proponents of international trade agreements governing intellectual property rights, Australia may well set the tone of patent legislation being designed in developing nations seeking to become compliant with TRIPS and join the World Trade Organization. Other nations may look to them as a role model for creating patent laws concerning human genetic material based not on reality or science or common sense, but purely on the desire to attract multinational corporations into doing business in their country. The case of Myriad Genetics has been long and complex. But in today's era of globalization, it is far from over.

References

Association for Molecular Pathology v. Myriad Genetics, Inc. (2013, June 13). *United States Supreme Court*. Full syllabus, opinion, and concurrence: http://supreme.justia.com/cases/federal/us/569/12-398/

"Australian federal court rules isolated genetic material can be patented." (2014, September 4). *The Guardian*. http://www.theguardian.com/world/2014/sep/05/court-rules-breast-cancer-gene-brca1-patented-australia

Bosch, Xavier. (2004, May 29). "Myriad loses rights to breast cancer gene patent." *Lancet, 363*(9423), 1780-1780.

Cancer Voices Australia v. Myriad Genetics Inc [2013] FCA 65. (2013, February 15). *Federal Court of Australia*. Full text including corrigendum added 25 February: http://www.judgments.fedcourt.gov.au/judgments/Judgments/fca/single/2013/2013fca0065

Cong Yao. (2012). "Federal circuit holds isolated DNA is patent-eligible—Association for Molecular Pathology v. United States Patent and Trademark Office (Myriad III)." *American Journal of Law & Medicine, (38)*4, 755-757.

Conley, John. (2010, June 21). "Myriad gene patent litigation goes down under." *Genomics Law Report*. http://www.genomicslawreport.com/index.php/2010/06/21/myriad-litigation-goes-down-under/

Cook-Deegan, Robert. (2014, September 30). "Australian

appeals court upholds patents on isolated BRCA1 DNA." *Genomics Law Report.* http://www.genomicslawreport.com/index.php/2014/0 9/30/australian-appeals-court-upholds-patents-on-isolated-brca1-dna/#more-13366

Cook-Deegan, Robert. (2013, August 20). "Are human genes patentable?" *Annals of Internal Medicine, 159*(4), 298-300.

Corderoy, Amy. (2014, September 5). "Mutation of breast cancer gene can be patented, says Federal Court." *The Sydney Morning Herald.* http://www.smh.com.au/national/health/mutation-of-breast-cancer-gene-can-be-patented-says-federal-court-20140905-10ckfp.html

D'Arcy v. Myriad Genetics Inc [2014] FCAFC 115 (2014, September 5). *Federal Court of Australia.* http://www.austlii.edu.au/au/cases/cth/FCAFC/2014/11 5.html

Gold, Richard, Carbone, Julia. (2010, April). "Myriad Genetics: In the eye of the policy storm." *Genetics in Medicine, 12*(4) Suppl., S39-S70. doi:10.1097/GIM.0b013e3181d72661 http://www.nature.com/gim/journal/v12/n1s/full/gim2 010142a.html

Leal, R. (2014, Spring). "The next step in gene patents: Association for Molecular Pathology v. Myriad Genetics." *Journal of Art, Technology & Intellectual Property Law, 24*(2), 403-423.

Masnick, Mike. (2014, September 9). "Australian court

disagrees with US: Claim genes are totally patentable."
TechDirt.
https://www.techdirt.com/articles/20140905/16275828
438/australian-court-disagrees-with-us-claim-genes-
are-totally-patentable.shtml

"Myriad diagnostic concerns." [Editorial]. (2013, July).
Nature Biotechnology, *31*(7), 571. doi:10.1038/nbt.2638

O'Neill, Graeme. (2009, April 3). "Jacobson speaks: Genetic
Technologies and BRCA testing." *Australian Life
Scientist*.
http://lifescientist.com.au/content/molecular-
biology/article/jacobson-speaks-genetic-technologies-
and-brca-testing-1127244197

"Patent Act of 1952—Patentable Subject Matter—Ass'n for
Molecular Pathology v. Myriad Genetics, Inc. (2013,
November)." *Harvard Law Review*, *127*(1), 388-407.

Rogers, Douglas L. (2013). "After Prometheus, are human
genes patentable subject matter?" *Duke Law &
Technology Review*, *11*(2), 434-508.

Shah, A. K., Warsh, J., Kesselheim, A. (2013, Winter). "The
ethics of intellectual property rights in an era of
globalization." *Journal of Law, Medicine & Ethics*, *41*(4),
841-851. doi:10.1111/jlme.12094

"Supreme Court orders new review of Myriad gene
patents." (2012, April/May). *GeneWatch*, *25*(3), 26.

"A Victory for Genes." [Editorial]. (2013, July). *Nature
Medicine*, *19*(7), 792. doi:10.1038/nm.3279

Patents and Public Health in the Age of TRIPS:
Why the Future Depends on Connecting Patent Offices with Public Health Agencies

Abstract

Conflicts between public health and the commercial interests of multinational pharmaceutical companies have come to the forefront of TRIPS criticism in light of recent health crises, including viral outbreaks and HIV. Multinational pharmaceutical companies played a significant role in creating TRIPS. They use its provisions to apply for patents in developing nations. The patents give them legal rights to control the supply of that medicine in that country, something public health agencies often confront only after it is too late. Ironically, TRIPS regulations do contain many provisions that developing nations could invoke to protect public health, provisions called flexibilities. However, these flexibilities may never make it into the country's legislation due to both a lack of resources in developing nations and pressure on patent offices to generate revenue by approving applications. Political pressures coerce nations to create TRIPS-based regulation granting pharmaceutical companies far more control than the nation needs to. In this high-powered, high-pressure global arena of TRIPS legislation, public health agencies desperately need to connect with patent offices to take a more influential role in developing and enforcing TRIPS regulations for their country. Administrative challenges faced by the patent offices also deserve attention, for the resources at the patent office in a developing nation do not equal those of developed nations. Therefore, the future of public health depends on the ability of patent offices around the world to achieve parity with the systems and resources of developed nations, and to connect in meaningful ways with public health agencies to fully evaluate the health implications of TRIPS legislation.

Keywords: Agreement on Trade-Related Aspects of Intellectual Property Rights, Doha Declaration, ethics, flexibilities, HIV/AIDS, intellectual property, international trade agreement, medicine, multinational pharmaceutical company, patent, patent office, pharmaceuticals, public administration, public health, TRIPS, TRIPS-plus, World Trade Organization.

I. Medicine as Intellectual Property.

The acronym TRIPS refers to an international trade agreement called the Agreement on Trade-Related Aspects of Intellectual Property Rights. It covers "patents, copyrights, trademarks, industrial design, and trade secrets" (Goodwin, 2008, p. 570). Led by the United States, the European Union, and Japan, a coalition of developed nations created TRIPS in 1994. "Intense lobbying by large multinationals including Pfizer, IBM, and Monsanto" helped shape the U.S. position on the agreement which focused on pharmaceuticals, software, agriculture, and entertainment products (Halbert, 2005). The U.S. during the Clinton Administration identified its copyright-based industries as its major exports and revenue generators, moving away from an earlier era of supremacy in manufacturing (Sum, 2003, p. 377). Given this period of history saw the rise of the North American Free Trade Agreement (NAFTA) and concerns over manufacturing jobs moving to other countries with cheaper labor, this historical shift to focusing on intellectual property should come as no surprise. The creation of TRIPS coincides with the creation of the World Trade Organization (WTO) in 1995 (Sum, 2003, p. 378). Ratifying the TRIPS agreement is now a condition for a nation to belong to the WTO and enjoy the free-trade benefits of membership. TRIPS aims to standardize protection of intellectual property rights among all WTO member nations (Shah p. 841).

What is intellectual property? The World Intellectual Property Organization (WIPO) defines intellectual property as "creations of the mind, such as inventions; literary and artistic works; designs; and symbols, names and images used in commerce" (WIPO, 2014). Though somewhat vague, this definition appears more concrete than some. Even in college classrooms today, students may learn that intellectual property "is the product of your research, hard work, and imagination" (Lanning, 2012, p.82). But such vague definitions raise many questions. If a man works hard to dig a ditch, is the ditch a form of intellectual property? Few would argue in favor of that proposition, even if the man had to perform research about where to dig and what tools to use. Intellectual property must be somehow distinguishable from physical, tangible property. The WIPO definition comes closest to defining where the difference lies and what the term covers. Even so, exactly what constitutes intellectual property, and to what extent anyone owns it, remains a point of contention.

Members of the WTO find themselves, under TRIPS, obliged to issue patents to protect pharmaceuticals as simply another form of property, like other forms of technology (Walker, 2001, p. 112). The inclusion of medicines in TRIPS as just another form of intellectual property—like a business logo, a fictional character, or even this essay—has caused the most widespread criticism and dispute of TRIPS. While other technologies such as software have given rise to disputes as well, access to medicine by the sick and poor in developing nations has caused the most outspoken response to TRIPS by governments, academics, and human rights groups around the world.

In terms of medicine, the claim that a newly synthesized medicine should become intellectual property remains open to debate. From the methods and equipment used in the research and development of the medicine to the previous research which provided a basis for it, the creation of a new medicine relies on the prior work of others. "The intellectual labor that went into the drug design process did not occur from first principles; rather, in every case, the inventor's thought process was critically shaped by the cumulative insights of his or her predecessors" (Shah, p. 844). To arrive at the final step and then claim total ownership appears to ignore history and the work of others.

In fact, the notion that property rights can apply to any idea at all remains open to debate. Taking another person's car, or house, or tools, or any real, physical object deprives the person of their use. But, recognizing a good idea and using it for oneself does not impede the originator's use of that same idea (Hilton, 2005, p. 72). Many people can enjoy the use of a good idea without detracting from any other person's use of that idea. While shoelaces may be considered a person's property, it would seem ridiculous to patent the idea of tying one's shoelaces to demand payments from every person who ties their shoelaces in the future. Many TRIPS-related agreements accomplish just that, only in terms of medicine. They even cover any future uses one might discover for the medicines, as if one could also patent every future use people might later invent for shoelaces beyond affixing shoes to one's feet.

The application of intellectual property law to medicines under TRIPS has caused conflict. The key disputes have come from nations affected by viral outbreaks, especially HIV/AIDS, which found themselves at the economic mercy of the patent holders of the necessary medicines. Multinational pharmaceutical companies hold these patents, and the disputes brought against them have led to reinterpretations and evaluations of TRIPS. This essay will take a closer look at specific cases, their disputes, and their consequences.

II. Commercial Interest versus Public Health.

Multinational pharmaceutical companies led by interests in the U.S., the European Union, and Japan played a significant role in defining how TRIPS treats patents (Halbert, 2005). Prior to TRIPS, patent offices in some developing countries would not patent pharmaceuticals in order to keep down the cost of medicine, or they only allowed patents on the "process" of creating the medicine—not the product itself (Van Puymbroeck, 2010, p. 525). HIV/AIDS medicines can be relatively inexpensive to produce, but, under TRIPS, the multinational pharmaceutical corporations who hold the patents can drive the purchase price up to where developing nations cannot readily afford it. Rather than "free trade," this creates artificial scarcity.

However, TRIPS and its subsequent interpretations have shown some protections for public health. Compulsory licenses allow the use of patented medicines by the public health sector and circumvent the standard licensing regulations to deal with emergencies (ibid, p. 525). These licenses are issued under judicial and administrative review and must be for government use only, not for private gain.

"International political pressure" forced the WTO to reconsider TRIPS in light of the growing spread of HIV/AIDS in developing countries and specifically in Africa (Halbert, 2005). This resulted in the Doha Declaration, which sought to clarify that nothing about TRIPS—regardless of its language—should be construed as constraining governments from taking measures to protect public health (Van Puymbroeck, 2010, p. 526). Formally known as the Declaration on the TRIPS Agreement and Public Health, this 2001 document from the WTO states that "the TRIPS agreement does not and should not prevent members from taking measures to protect public health," and that the interpretation and implementation of TRIPS should support "WTO members' right to protect public health and, in particular, to promote access to medicines for all" (Kobori, 2002, p. 11).

Multinational pharmaceutical corporations such as GlaxoSmithKline voice opposition to the government-forced compulsory licenses mandated during public health crises. These compulsory licenses stifle innovation, according to the Pharmaceutical Research and Manufacturers of America (PhrMA) (Van Puymbroeck, 2010, p. 525). However, counter arguments include criticisms that the TRIPS system has also failed to innovate medicines for developing countries. The World Health Organization's 2006 report, issued by its Commission on Innovation, Intellectual Property, and Public Health, found that when people and nations are too poor to purchase medicines for diseases that are killing millions of people, patents do not encourage research, development, and innovations to bring new medicines to that market (Outterson, 2008, p. 279). If a country has no money for research and development, this report proposes, then it will fail to innovate its own medicines for its own health crises. And if it has no money, such a country offers no financial incentive to more wealthy nations to develop and sell medicines to it. After all, few companies innovate products for people who cannot pay for them. A market must exist for innovations to arise from profit motives, and the infrastructure must exist to make innovation possible.

Another argument supporting the contentions of the pharmaceutical companies relates to their ability to recoup the cost of bringing the medicines to market. However, sales of medicines in developed countries, whose wealthier populations can generally afford higher-priced medicines, compensate for lower revenues from developing nations (Walker, 2001, p. 111). Few would argue the corporations in question should lose money to develop medicines, but inflating prices in developing nations is not the only solution available to them. Moreover, developing nations only generate a relatively small amount of profits for pharmaceutical companies compared to developed nations. As of 2008, eighty to ninety percent of global sales of patented medicines came from the thirty wealthiest nations in the Organization for Economic Cooperation and Development, suggesting that if "developing countries cannot currently afford the drugs... pharmaceutical companies are not foregoing any revenue by providing the drugs at generic prices" (Goodwin, 2008, p. 576).

Is it really the high cost of medicines that prevents them from reaching the poor people who need them most? The patent lawyers for these pharmaceutical companies have issued statements that lack of money and infrastructure in developing countries, not the patents, interfere with distribution of medicine (Van Puymbroeck, 2010, p. 525). But UNAIDS, the United Nations organization that studies and treats HIV/AIDS worldwide, found the "patents that allow exclusive control over the manufacture, import, and sale" do play a role in creating high prices for treatments, and these high prices necessarily restrict the poor's access to the medicines (Walker, 2001, p. 110). The World Health Organization found high cost presented "one of the major obstacles to providing access to essential medications in developing countries," and the U.S. Government Accountability Office notes that developing nations may "spend as much as seventy percent of their health care budgets on medication" compared to fifteen percent or less in developed nations (Goodwin, 2008, p. 570). Few can doubt the patents relate to high costs, and high costs relate to a lack of access to the medicines in developing nations.

However, patents and high cost cannot unilaterally bear the blame for the problems in distributing medicines to the sick and the poor in developing nations. In developing nations, many people live far away from hospitals, society lacks sufficient training for doctors, and governments may be corrupt and dysfunctional—all of which contributes to a lack of access to even the inexpensive medicines (Dutfield, 2008, p. 108). The Center for International Development surveyed fifty-three countries in Africa to identify where patents existed for fifteen antiretroviral medicines used in HIV/AIDS treatment. Published in the *Journal of the American Medical Association* in 2001, the survey found that few of the countries had issued patent protection for these medicines, and the existing patents mostly stemmed from three companies: Pfizer, GlaxoSmithKline, and Boehringer Ingelheim (Kobori, 2002, p. 13).

Counterarguments from nongovernmental organizations questioned this survey. They pointed out it ignored many significant products that had, in fact, been patented in those countries, and that surveying only fifteen medicines out of "a potential 795 drugs, or combinations of drugs" gave a woefully inadequate picture of the true situation (ibid, p. 13). It might serve the commercial interest of multinational pharmaceutical corporations to place the blame anywhere but on their revenue-generating patents, but it is true patents are not the only obstacle to distributing medicines in the developing nations of the world. Patents are, however, a contributing factor, and they are one that public administration can address.

Compulsory licenses and the Doha Declaration aside, TRIPS member nations have other flexibilities available to protect public health and set their own standards for what gets patented and what does not (Correa, 2001, p. 79). Why many nations fail to fully utilize these flexibilities will be the subject of later sections of this essay. However, it is worth noting here that TRIPS member nations, as members of the World Trade Organization, enjoy some rights to combat "abuses" of intellectual property control. For example, the Competition Commission of South Africa won licenses for four companies to produce AIDS medicine as recourse to price gouging by GlaxoSmithKline and Boehringer Ingelheim (Van Puymbroeck, 2010, p. 527). The WTO, as both enforcer and evaluator of TRIPS and its disputes, has simultaneously set the stage for these abuses to arise due to commercial interests, and also created the arena in which they may be resolved in favor of public health.

The Doha Declaration and the TRIPS flexibilities gave rise to Canada's 2005 adoption of the Jean Chretién Pledge to Africa, an amendment to Canada's patent laws now known as Canada's Access to Medicines Regime (CAMR) (Goodwin, 2008, p. 569). The Doha Declaration ordered the TRIPS Council to remedy the restrictions that TRIPS Article 31 placed on governments desiring to apply for compulsory licenses to distribute patented medicines during health crises. Article 31 limited governments to medicines their domestic markets could supply, something that proved a major obstacle in nations lacking research and development facilities and funding to even have such domestic market. The TRIPS Council created a remedy in Paragraph 6 which dealt with the export of patented medicines to countries who faced challenges creating their own medicines domestically. Canada "became the first country to authorize the manufacture of generic medications under the Paragraph 6 Division when it authorized Apotex, Inc. to manufacture 260,000 packs of

TriAvir (in generic form, ApoTriavir,) an HIV/AIDS medication, for export to Rwanda" (ibid, p. 569).

The Canadian example demonstrates the potential for public administrators to bring public health to the forefront when creating or modifying their patent laws. Certainly the commercial interest of the authorized manufacturer plays a role, but CAMR shows a potential to break the stranglehold patent-holding multinationals exert on a developing nations' government. As the patent office section of this paper will discuss, multinational pharmaceutical companies have often blocked a government's ability to manufacture and distribute generic versions of HIV/AIDS medicines. Removing these blocks can mean a lengthy and costly legal battle for the affected nation. CAMR shows one way out of this trap: the export of generic medicines by a more developed nation to a less developed one. Norway, for example, soon followed Canada's lead by amending their patent laws governing compulsory licenses in such a way that "the King may by regulations prescribe rules that deviate from" only issuing compulsory licenses to supply their own domestic market, and seven other WTO member nations subsequently "amended their patent laws to allow for the export of generic medication under Paragraph 6" (ibid, p.577).

CAMR was not without its criticisms, however, and public administrators should be aware of them. For example, the list of drugs and vaccines covered by CAMR only contained fifty-seven medications, mostly HIV/AIDS related, many of which already had generic competitors or were not covered by patents (Outterson, 2008, p. 282). If the goal was alleviating the lack of access to patented medicines and their generic forms, then Canada's Access to Medicines Regimes may not have taken things far enough.

Furthermore, Canada has a lengthy review process for

medicines, and this applies to medicines created for export, not simply their own domestic use (Goodwin, 2008, p. 578). This lengthy review process, combined with a somewhat complex application process for a nation requesting the generic medications, may limit Canada from getting medicines prepared for export in a timely fashion when confronted with a health crisis. Finally, the multinational pharmaceutical companies holding the patents may also have recourse to opposing these measures. Fortunately, for thousands of Rwandans, GlaxoSmithKline did not oppose the distribution of ApoTriavir in this case and also agreed to "waive royalty payments it would otherwise be entitled to under CAMR... on the condition that medication is supplied on a not-for-profit basis" (ibid, p. 575).

The Canadian Access to Medicines Regime, though imperfect, demonstrates how a developed nation can take action, even in this age of TRIPS, to provide assistance to developing nations. The future of public health depends on this good will, for the inequities in resources, infrastructure, and money between developed and developing nations suggest that developing nations cannot achieve all they need on their own. The governments and governmental agencies of developed nations will need to help less-developed nations by giving priority to their humanitarian and public health concerns. In addition, the patent offices of developed nations will need to bridge the gaps of inequity to help the patent offices and public health agencies in the developing world achieve parity in their systems, resources, and expertise. Many failures of developing nations to adequately address public health under their TRIPS regulations stem from inability to evaluate and administer their regulations and patent offices effectively. The next sections of this essay will examine how these inequities affect, in practical terms, the operations of patent offices around the world and lead to public health crises.

III. The Consequence of Inequities between Nations.

Inequities in wealth and resources between developed and developing nations cause concern that the poorest nations will be exploited by the stronger ones. TRIPS and similar intellectual property controls cause fear their aim is not stimulating innovation but giving the dominant players from developed nations the power to make all human thought and knowledge into commodities, and to profit from this at the expense of nations and peoples (Häyrinen-Alestalo, 2001, p. 207). In the field of public health, this fear takes a specific form. People fear that multinational pharmaceutical companies and their interests in developed nations will use patents to control their medicines. Then, the companies gain a position where they can set any price they choose, and gouge the poorer countries to pay for medicine at artificially high prices. Also, the patents can prevent the use of medicines developed in competing labs independently of the patent-holder. And the patents can prevent governments from creating and distributing less expensive generic medicines to their people. All these fears have basis in fact, as they have already come to pass.

Critics argue the stronger, more developed nations forced TRIPS on developing nations that did not yet have the infrastructure and resources to be ready for it (Van Puymbroeck, 2010, p. 525). However, the least developed nations had an extended time to adopt TRIPS: as late as 2013 for most of the regulation and until January 1, 2016 for pharmaceutical patents. Despite this extension, countries often find themselves coerced into accepting stricter regulations than the standard TRIPS agreement before gaining entry as a member nation.

Even when nations voluntarily choose to adopt more

than the minimum standards of TRIPS, these TRIPS-plus agreements can place more value on intellectual property rights than public health. For example, the Australia-United States Free Trade Agreement (AUFSTA) contained proposed modifications to TRIPS. Critics pointed out that AUFSTA "potentially limits compulsory licensing for 'failure to work,'" and possibly restricts "the opportunity for Australia to rely on the 'flexibility' to implement laws that 'protect public health and nutrition'" (Lawson, 2004, p. 357). AUFSTA also proposed to expressly require patents for "any new uses or methods of using a known product" (ibid, p. 358).

In terms of medicines or medical treatments, this would extend patent control over any new way of using an existing product. This practice resembles patenting aspirin, then patenting its use to relieve headaches, and then separately patenting its use to reduce fever, and insisting on patent protection for every possible use subsequently discovered. Many medicines developed to alleviate depression have shown this ability to be repurposed, for example. Through clinical trials, a number of anti-depressants have also proven effective for smoking cessation, obesity reduction, and other uses (Shah, 2013, p. 846). TRIPS-plus regulations like the ones proposed in Australia would seek to extend intellectual property rights to cover all these new uses. Despite allowing for compulsory licenses in a national emergency, these AUFSTA propositions clearly sought even more restrictive control over the flexibilities and licenses that directly affect public health. They aim to attract foreign investment and technology with stronger intellectual property rights at the expense of protections for public health.

TRIPS has raised concerns that stronger nations have gained the power to monopolize information and innovation at the expense of poorer countries. Developing nations may simply adopt TRIPS without modification, or copy developed nations' intellectual property laws because they lack the resources to draft and evaluate their own effective legislation. In 2005, the World Health Organization reported many developing nations have not taken advantage of the maximum flexibilities allowed under the Doha interpretation. This means that developing nations have not taken full advantage of all the protections available to them.

Why not? They may not have the resources and expertise to do something about it. Complying with TRIPS patent regulations means developing nations bear the cost of catching up with more developed patent offices. Developing nations bear this cost while also bearing the brunt of payments on patents, a cost in the billions of dollars worldwide as money flows from poorer countries to richer ones. Just in the field of software, for example, the organization Free and Open Source Software for Africa calculated that as of 2004, sub-Saharan countries paid "$24 billion each year to (mainly US-based) software companies to secure the use of proprietary products" (May 2006, p. 123). A full implementation of TRIPS could, by some economists' calculations, result in $40 billion in increased patent payments to the United States, Germany, Japan, France, the United Kingdom, and Switzerland (Van Puymbroeck, 2010, p. 529).

Policy makers need to consider how this economic imbalance determines which companies gain dominance over others and how it affects international trade negotiations. Patent litigation is a costly process that drives out smaller competitors who may have legitimate claims but cannot afford the lengthy trials. Fighting a competitor in court takes money. Even a favorable outcome in a trial can be a pyrrhic victory at best, with court costs and lawyer fees turning into an expense that dwarfs any gains the winning party might have made. In the U.S., many people know how Microsoft squeezed out competitors though patent litigation in the early days of their rise to prominence. On an international level, researchers and companies in poorer countries face the risk of being squeezed out by powerful multinationals in similar disputes. A plea for these nations to settle their disputes in courts really does little to protect their interests.

IV. Problems and Power at the Patent Offices.

For patent offices around the world, the ethical and conceptual concerns raised by TRIPS become practical, administrative concerns. Even before TRIPS, the three major patent offices in the world—the Trilateral of the U.S., Europe, and Japan—had already progressed towards a unified, global system of patent administration. Acting as hubs for patent information, the Trilaterals had improved their data systems for reviewing new applications and searching for prior ones, and then gradually opened these systems for access by other patent offices around the world (Drahos, 2008, p. 155).

But even though the information hub exists, not all the spokes connect to it equally due to their local limitations. In *"Trust Me": Patent Office in Developing Countries*, Peter Drahos writes of his visits to patent offices in the Philippines, Laos, and Indonesia. He found people moving boxes of paper files from one floor to another to make photocopies, five workers sharing a single desktop computer, and whole offices waiting for computers to arrive just so they could get up and running (ibid, p. 159). These examples highlight the inequities in resources between developed and developing nations. Even if the most powerful nations on earth are ready for TRIPS, their less developed neighbors may struggle to achieve an equal footing.

The lack of resources creates opportunities for multinationals to apply for patents in nations which lack the infrastructure to evaluate the potential effects of issuing the patent. For example, registering an HIV treatment in a developing nation might prevent the government from using less expensive generic treatments for major public health crises. This is not a purely hypothetical concern.

In 1998, the patent office in Thailand issued Bristol-Meyers Squibb a patent on Dideoxy Purine Nucleosides, a form of the medicine didanosine. Didanosine is, in simple terms, a medicine used to treat HIV. The World Health Organization includes it on their *List of Essential Medicines* (WHO, 2013, p. 12). The patent protection forced Thailand's Government Pharmaceutical Organization to stop manufacturing their generic version of the medicine. Six years of litigation and campaigning by the government and citizens of Thailand resulted only in Bristol-Meyers Squibb withdrawing the patent. The courts never ruled on it and therefore established no legal precedent to deal with similar patents in the future (Drahos, 2008, p. 166). This case illustrates the pitfalls of pressuring patent offices to handle applications from multinational pharmaceutical companies regardless of their ability to evaluate potential public health concerns.

Yet the local patent offices are not without powers of their own. In fact, they have significant power to affect the course of international trade agreements like TRIPS and even the resulting patent litigation. In the Thailand case, the patent office "came under criticism because it intervened in ways that favoured Bristol-Meyers Squibb" (ibid, p. 167). Why would the patent office try to sway the court case in Bristol-Meyers Squibb's favor? One might suspect pressure to generate revenue. The patent offices collect fees, and a wave of multinational pharmaceuticals registering in Thailand would generate potentially significant revenue.

Local patent offices also play an influential role in negotiating trade agreements like TRIPS and TRIPS-plus. They often provide the negotiating expertise for developing countries which have trade negotiations with more developed countries, especially where intellectual property comes into play. They take an active role in "interpreting, advising, and negotiating standards of patent protection" (ibid, p. 162-3). Patent offices could, if they wished, exercise power protectively by denying patents so their country can reverse-engineer the innovations (ibid, p. 169). But more often than not, to the detriment of public health, the patent office accepts the application fee and issues the patent to the multinational pharmaceutical company.

That local patent offices have a pro-patent bias comes as no surprise. To protect their revenue, they have a financial incentive to oppose any initiatives that question how they issue patents. They gain power to do this because they have access to resources of the patent offices of developed countries, and because their work is so technical that the public cannot easily evaluate it (ibid, p. 163). But financial self-interest alone does not account for all actions of a patent office. The sheer volume of patent applications globally tends to focus the system on issuing patents quickly and efficiently, not necessarily the quality of the results for public health.

Neither the challenges nor the powers of patent offices are clear to public health officials, who often have no interaction with them until after the medical patent becomes a problem. Patent offices do not often connect with the offices of public health in their country. Many health officials have no knowledge of how their local patent offices work or what they currently have for review. Only communication between public health departments and the patent offices during the patent reviews can bridge the gap.

Patent offices enjoy other powers built into the additional flexibilities of TRIPS. They may refuse patents on surgical and diagnostic techniques, therapeutic methods, and any inventions which, when used commercially, would threaten public health. They may also refuse to patent plants and animals.

The patenting of plants and animals was once not possible even in the U.S., owing to a 1948 Supreme Court decision in *Funk Brothers Seed Co. v. Kalo Inoculant Co.* The court ruled that "simply combining several existing species of bacteria into one product was not patentable because all of the components of the invention were known and naturally occurring" (Leal, 2014, p. 407). Subsequent court decisions in the United States overturned this precedent by granting patentability to specific genes and even multicellular organisms (ibid, p. 408).

Now, TRIPS flexibilities allow the courts of other nations to make this decision on their own, rather than merely copy the U.S. This flexibility has more to do with agriculture and genetically modified organisms than medicine; but it affects public health to the extent these living things serve as food for humans and livestock.

A sophisticated understanding of TRIPS and its flexibilities ideally informs a nation's public health agencies about steps they can take to protect the public. An example from India demonstrates that developing nations need not consider sophisticated use of flexibilities a lost cause. Prior to TRIPS, many of the Indian companies developing medicines were not solely profit-driven companies. This did not change despite India's need to pass intellectual property laws that complied with TRIPS to gain membership in the WTO (Bhattacharya, 2008, p. 396). India created a speedy process for applications for compulsory licenses, an administrative move that placed the needs of the sick and the poor above commercial interests in times of public health crises. India's Patent Act, ratified in 2005 as part of their TRIPS-related regulations, took into account the development of

HIV/AIDS medicines before joining the WTO, addressing the problem proactively instead of waiting for costly legal disputes or public outcry.

While as imperfect as any of the measures discussed in this essay, the India example suggests that even in the age of TRIPS, public health can play just as important a role as commercial interests in a nation's approach to intellectual property and medicine. Patent offices and public health agencies must fully consider the flexibilities available to them, and look for ways to draft legislation that truly serves the public. TRIPS is heavily skewed in favor of the multinational pharmaceutical companies, but that does not mean a nation must accept exploitation.

Developing nations will need help and support from developed nations to realize this goal effectively. This seems only fair, as the pressure to accept and implement TRIPS comes from those same developed nations that could best help their global neighbors protect their people. In an age of increasingly deadly viral outbreaks and new diseases, the future of public health depends on this helpful and humanitarian approach that prioritizes people over profit, a world view that promotes assistance over exploitation.

V. The Future of Patent Offices and Public Health.

Researchers and administrators face a common problem: understanding the scope and effect of TRIPS requires additional knowledge of international trade agreements that have sought to clarify or expand TRIPS. TRIPS establishes baseline standards; but, many nations have created expanded agreements, often called TRIPS-Plus or TRIPS+.

Consider just a few examples. The 1996 World Intellectual Property Organization Copyright Treaty (WIPO) aimed at reducing circumvention of Digital Rights Management (DRM) protection. In the field of arts and entertainment, broadcasters and webcasters sought rights over their broadcasts by campaigning for a WIPO Broadcasting Treaty in addition to TRIPS regulations. The European Union in 2001 created a Copyright Directive aimed at more enforcement of patent laws than TRIPS provided.

The proliferation of these extended agreements demonstrates the tip of the iceberg of regulations and paperwork someone faces when attempting to learn about TRIPS and its consequences. In this atmosphere of information overload, developing nations may lack the legal and technical resources to draft their own legislation. They often resort to copying the laws of more developed nations.

The future global unification of patent offices will require public administrators to integrate systems from many nations and standardize application processes. The future of patent offices will show a merger of the administrative systems, not just cooperation between offices. This will look like centralized application systems and globally-standardized forms. This future will require nations with technologically and organizationally more efficient systems to help other nations improve and integrate their patent operations into the new global system.

As the patent offices of developing nations around the world bring their administrative systems up to the same level of technology and efficiency as developed nations and the Trilateral patent offices, they will need the support of developed nations. The European Patent Office (EPO) provides one example of how to accomplish this. Their International Academy, begun in 1977, "offers technical, administrative, and legal training to government officials, patent examiners, prosecutors, patent judges, and patent attorneys for member and future member states" (Sum, 2003, p. 379). Programs like this, focused on training and educating, will provide a critical piece of the puzzle that global standardization of intellectual property control has become.

Upgrading and interfacing technology systems presents challenges, but it also presents an opportunity. As these patent offices develop and grow, public health agencies have a chance to network and connect with them, and to make sure that public health concerns are given priority over commercial interests in their review process. Public health agencies must realize the time to address public health concerns is not after the fact of the patents, but before. Patent offices and public health agencies must reach across the administrative boundaries between their operations to form a unified front against exploitation of their nations by the multinational pharmaceutical companies. In the face of the ongoing HIV/AIDS crisis and the threat of uncontrolled viral outbreaks, the very future of public health depends on their ability to work together, not against each other.

References

Bhattacharya, R. (2008). "Are developing countries going too far on TRIPS? A closer look at the new laws in India." *American Journal of Law & Medicine, 34*(2/3), 395-421.

Correa, C. M. (2001, January). "The TRIPS agreement: How much room for maneuver?" *Journal of Human Development, 2*(1), 79-107. doi:10.1080/14649880120050192

Drahos, P. (2008). "Trust me: Patent offices in developing countries." *American Journal of Law & Medicine, 34*(2/3), 151-174.

Dutfield, G. (2008). "Delivering drugs to the poor: Will the TRIPS amendment help?" *American Journal of Law & Medicine, 34*(2/3), 107-124.

Goodwin, P. E. (2008). "Right idea, wrong result— Canada's Access to Medicines Regime." *American Journal of Law & Medicine, 34*(4), 567-584.

Halbert, D. (2005). "Globalized resistance to intellectual property." *Globalization.* http://globalization.icaap.org/content/v5.2/halbert.html

Häyrinen-Alestalo, M. (2001, July). "Is knowledge-based society a relevant strategy for civil society?" *Current Sociology, 49*(4), 203-218. doi:10.1177/0011392101049004011

Hilton, J. (2005). "In praise of sharing." *EDUCAUSE*

Review, 40(3), 72-73.

Kobori, S. (2002, May). "TRIPS and the primacy of public health." *Asia-Pacific Review, 9*(1), 10-19. doi:10.1080/13439000220141550

Lanning, S. (2012). *Concise guide to information literacy.* Santa Barbara, CA: ABC-CLIO, LLC.

Lawson, C. and Pickering, C. (2004, December). "TRIPs-Plus patent privileges—An intellectual property 'cargo cult' in Australia." *Prometheus, 22*(4), 355-377. doi:10.1080/08109020412331311632

Leal, R. (2014, Spring). "The next step in gene patents: Association for Molecular Pathology v. Myriad Genetics." *Journal of Art, Technology & Intellectual Property Law, 24*(2), 403-423.

Lopert, R., Gleeson, D. (2013, Spring). "The high price of 'free' trade: U.S. trade agreements and access to medicines." *Journal of Law, Medicine & Ethics, 41*(1), 199-223. doi:10.1111/jlme.12014

May, C. (2006, March). "Escaping the TRIPs' trap: The political economy of free and open source software in Africa." *Political Studies, 54*(1), 123-146. doi:10.1111/j.1467-9248.2006.00569.x

Outterson, K. (2008). "Should access to medicines and TRIPS flexibilities be limited to specific diseases?" *American Journal of Law & Medicine, 34*(2/3), 279-301.

Shah, A. K., Warsh, J., Kesselheim, A. (2013, Winter). "The ethics of intellectual property rights in an era of globalization." *Journal of Law, Medicine & Ethics, 41*(4), 841-851. doi:10.1111/jlme.12094

Sum, N. (2003, September). "Informational capitalism and U.S. economic hegemony: Resistance and adaptations in East Asia." *Critical Asian Studies, 35*(3), 373-398.

Van Puymbroeck, R. V. (2010, Fall). "Basic survival needs and access to medicines—Coming to grips with TRIPS: conversion + calculation." *Journal of Law, Medicine & Ethics, 38*(3), 520-549. doi:10.1111/j.1748-720X.2010.00510.x

Walker, S. (2001). "The implications of TRIPS: Ethics, health, and human rights." *Journal of Human Development, 2*(1), 109-114. doi:10.1080/14649880120050200

(WHO) World Health Organization (2013, April). *WHO model list of essential medicines, 18th ed.* Retrieved November 20, 2014 from http://apps.who.int/iris/bitstream/10665/93142/1/EML _18_eng.pdf

(WIPO) World Intellectual Property Organization. "What is intellectual property?" http://www.wipo.int/about-ip/en/

About the Author

Matthew earned a Bachelor of Interdisciplinary Studies in Public Administration in 2014 from Northern Arizona University. He continues his studies at Fort Hays State University where he is working towards a Master of Liberal Studies in Public Administration. He studies public policy as it relates to patents, international trade agreements, health, and telecommunications in the Internet age. He also holds two degrees from Phoenix College, an Associate in General Business and an Associate in Marketing. He began self-publishing his own work in 2014. In addition to his public policy essays, Matthew has published a book of poetry and drawings, a dream journal, an ongoing science fiction adventure series, and two albums of original guitar music.

Matthew enjoys helping other authors self-publish their work. He supports authors, speakers, and business professionals in creating books that provide positive, practical information to improve people's lives and make a difference in our world. Their recent projects have contributed to greater awareness in the fields of business leadership, interpersonal communication, personal finance, and health & nutrition.

Having studied professional editing, technical writing, and document production management at the university level, Matthew brings many skills to these projects, from editing and interior design to the creation of Kindle-ready documents. He consults on all aspects of the writing and self-publishing process, and supports authors by helping them manage their book projects and production teams.

9780692367193